HEREFORD
Then & Now
Volume Two

by Derek Foxton

HEREFORD
Then . . . .

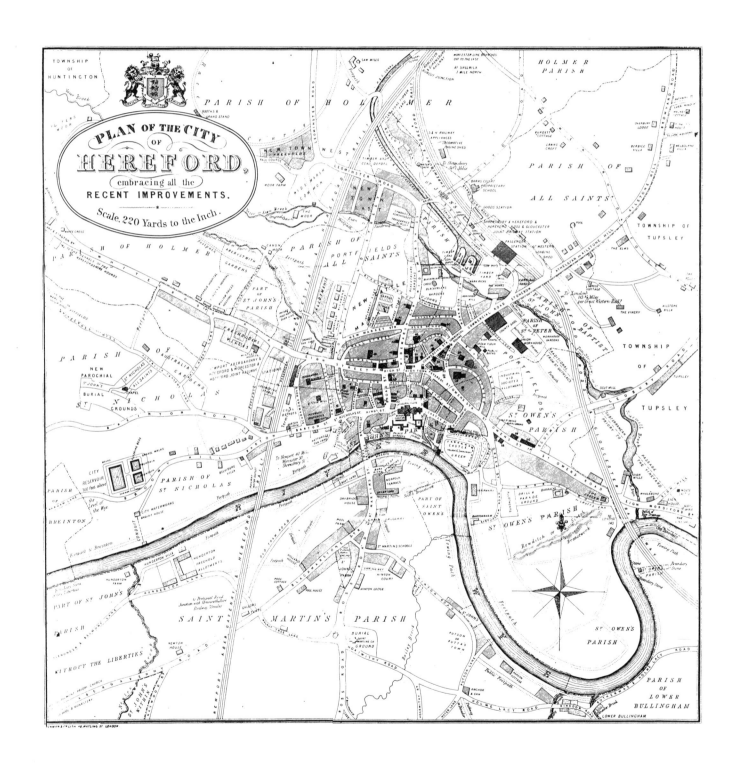

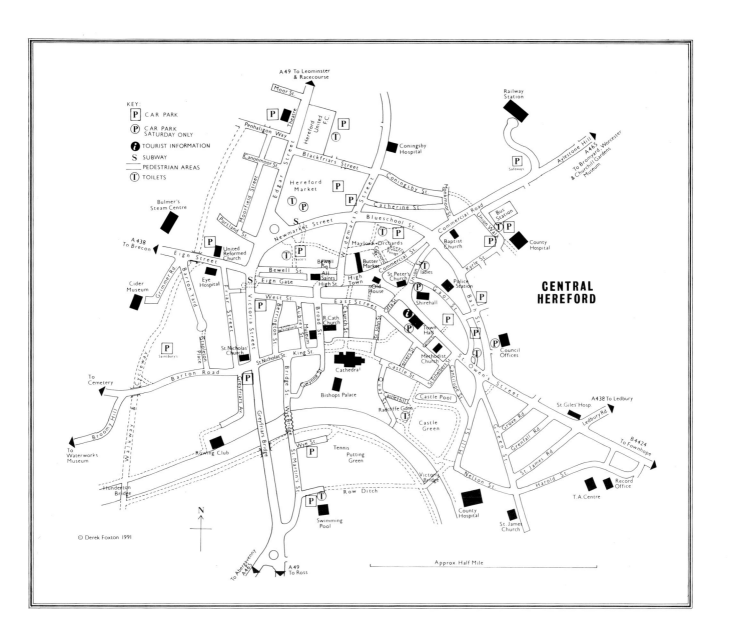

CENTRAL HEREFORD

© Derek Foxton 1991

Approx Half Mile

Published by
Derek Foxton
15a Commercial Street
Hereford
HR1 2DE
Telephone: 0432 269666

ISBN 0 9514081 1 9

Designed and produced by
Amber Graphics
Bideford House
Church Lane
Ledbury
Herefordshire
HR8 1DW

Printed by
The Bath Press, Bath

Introduction

Following the publication of *Hereford Then and Now* three years ago I have been asked by many people if there would be another volume. At first this was not possible because of a lack of interesting old photographs. Since then however, many people have brought their family pictures to my attention and I have been able to beg and borrow from many other sources. I hope that this book will become another record for future generations as well as be of interest to the present day reader.

The majority of changes in the city took place during the period 1950–1980 when planning laws were very flexible and not subject to the strict controls which exist today. In view of this many developers disregarded much of our heritage and took advantage of the lax laws to demolish virtually anything. We must remember that the local authorities were often powerless to prevent such destruction and thus should not always be blamed. So, in future years we may not see such major changes since local authority power and conservation area laws will preserve the best of our heritage as well as control future development, though no doubt we will still see new buildings and improvement alterations.

Much of our heritage is still undiscovered and the City Archaeology Unit has begun selected surveys in the central area, where they have made many interesting discoveries, which have included unknown early timber-framed buildings, some with painted plaster.

We cannot live in the past and where there are no special reasons to conserve, new buildings will be built but hopefully with well thought out designs. An example is the new W. H. Smith shop where there is a well preserved timber-framed building at the front, part of which is clearly visible by a glimpse at the ceiling. The rest of the store towards East Street is all new, while the new shop front is of a design that has received national attention.

In the residential areas of the city we now see alterations to houses built even fairly recently. Many wooden features, such as windows and doors are replaced when rot sets in. Plastic is often used for window frames with a pattern not similar to the old. Front doors are replaced with a version using tropical forest wood, and not in keeping with the original character. Owners who replace with materials and design similar to the original are to be congratulated.

Some of the old photographs used in this book were taken with very simple cameras and are not very sharp. However, because of their historical interest they have been reproduced where no other similar picture exists. If you have, or know of any, pictures similar to those in this book which would be suitable for another volume please send a description or photocopy to the author/publisher — one picture in this book came via Australia! Every effort has been made to ascertain copyright where necessary.

Derek Foxton
November 1991

Acknowledgements

I wish to express my thanks to my family, especially my wife Maria, daughters Dominique and Jessica, and mother Melanie for their help; to Basil Butcher for his help and advice over many years as well as checking the historical accuracy, and to the following:

Dr Farmer; John Smith, Managing Director Inco Ltd (page 66); 'Gallery Now'; the Teague family; Mrs M Brooks; Mrs Smith (page 30); Alex Dawson, Hereford Cider Museum (page 77); Graham Wrightson, c/o John Brunton Architect (page 54); Colin Quinsey (page 87); Sandra Green, Site Manager, County Hospital (page 83); Keith James, Bustin Collection; Sue Hubbard, Hereford Records Office (pages 40, 69); Mr M Paul, Manager, Marks & Spencer; The Dean, The Very Rev P Haines; The Rt Rev, The Bishop of Hereford; Mr Hexter, Manager, Midland Bank; Mike Davies, M D Helicopters, Hereford; Mrs Reynolds, 'Elmhurst', H&WCC; Mrs Doris Jenkins; Linda Appleyard, Quarry House; Major Brenda Tromans and Ken Farr, Salvation Army (page 29); Peggy Withington (pages 52, 53, 86, 88); Mrs S Hughson (page 27); Tim Ward (page 43), T E Dunabin, 'The Hereford Bus'; Mrs Lewin (pages 80, 81, 82, 84); Graham Roberts, 'Elgar and 250 Years of Three Choirs'; Robin Hill, Hereford Reference Library; Ann Sandford (page 76); The Hereford Times (page 59); John Sweetman (page 73); Miss Bantom sisters (page 18); Angus Jones (page 49); Peter Mountford (page 33); Mr R Johns (page 15); The Directors, W H Smith & Son (page 46); Mrs Prowlin, 'The Post Office History in Hereford'; John Chadd (page 44); Roy Massey; John Hodges (page 40); Brian Hornsby, '90 years of the Cinema in Hereford'; Rev Robert Harris (page 48); Midland Red; Alan Blake (page 79); Mrs King (page 62); Richard Hammonds (page 93); Roy Raithatha, Hereford Ice Cream Co; Mrs Evelyn Evans; Dave Stevens, Manager, and Karina Robbin, Rumbelows; David W Darts, Manager, Commercial Union Assurance; Les Forsbrook, Elgar Estates; Ron Shoesmith and Ken Hovard, Hereford Archaeology Committee (page 21); Mrs Jean O'Donnell (pages 58, 68, 72); Geoff Gwatkin, Cartographer; Hereford & Worcester County Council Social Services Dept (pages 64, 65); Peter Norman of Edwin John Photography; Syd Williams (page 12); Mr Waring (page 71); R L & E S Griffiths (page 34); A C E Weston (page 57); Mr P Pritchard, ARPS (pages 18, 74); Donovan Wilson (page 23); Jim Winters (page 92); Hereford Military Club; the Jelfs family (pages 36, 37); Mr Bettington (page 39); Harold Morgan (page 28); Hereford & Worcester County Council Youth Services (page 95); and David Postle.

Opposite top: Hereford Cathedral is of Norman origin, which replaced an earlier church that was totally destroyed in 1055 by Welsh invaders. The upper part of the bell tower was completed by 1369. The west end of the Cathedral was insecure for many years, and repairs were ineffective since it collapsed on Easter Monday April 17th 1786. The architect appointed by the Dean and Chapter to replace the west front was James Wyatt, who shortened the Cathedral by one bay or 15 feet, altered the pitch of the nave and transepts and constructed the triforium on the instructions of the Dean. The central tower spire was also removed at this time. During the 1840's much restoration was carried out including the underpinning of the tower foundations. In the 1860's Sir Gilbert Scott, architect, supervised further extensive repair and restoration. This picture postcard shows the old west front designed by Wyatt before alteration about 1897.

Opposite bottom: The old Wyatt west front was altered by architect Oldrid Scott at the turn of the century at a cost of £15,560. The changes are clearly visible. The west window was erected as a memorial to Queen Victoria and was unveiled by HRH Princess Henry of Battenberg on 13th May 1902. The new west front was considered a vast improvement and was dedicated by the Archbishop of Canterbury in 1904. The new building to the right is the Library which was built c1895 and was described at the time as the first absolutely new cathedral building since the North Porch. The tower corner is undergoing repairs, and the stonemasons hut is visible behind the tree.

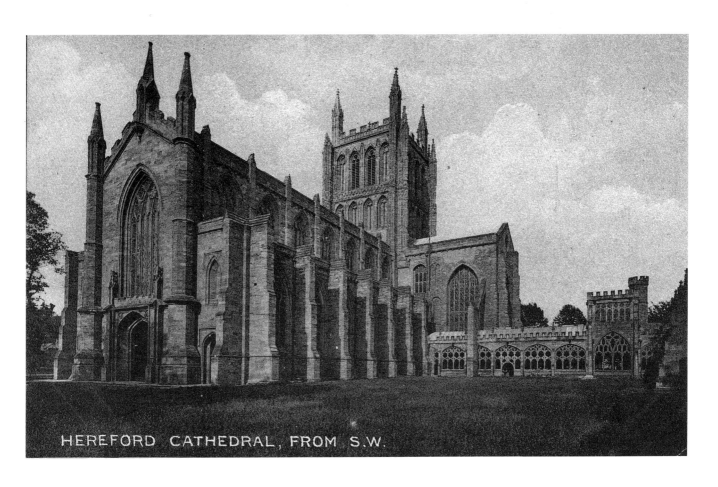

HEREFORD CATHEDRAL, FROM S.W.

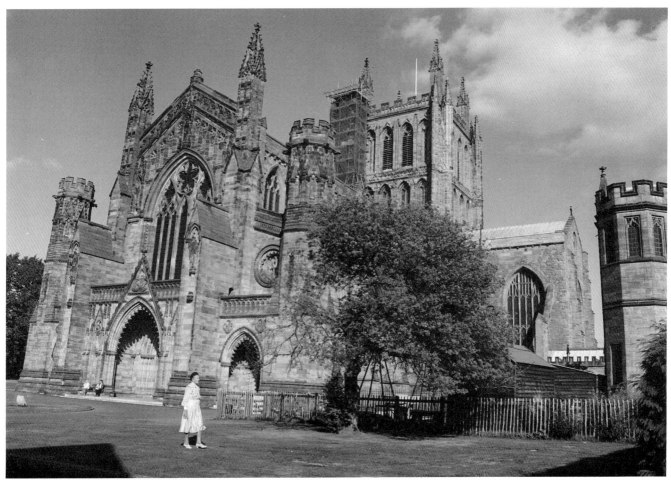

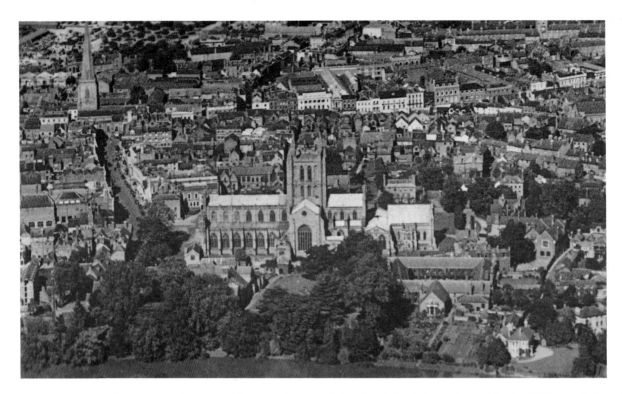

Hereford Cathedral has a prominent position on the north bank of the River Wye with the Bishops Palace in the foreground, surrounded by trees. The Cathedral with its high roof line and tall tower dominates the picture. The Lady Chapel seen to the right of the tower looks almost detached. The present structure originates from the Norman period and building started during the term of Bishop Reinhelm, 1107–1115. To the left of the cathedral is a view all along Broad Street with All Saints Church at the north end. The imposing facade of the buildings in High Town and Commercial Street are seen to the top right. This photograph, taken about 1935, shows a great deal of the city centre.

This photograph taken during the autumn of 1990 shows the River Wye in the foreground behind the mature trees with a clear view of the Bishops Palace. In Broad Street the roof of the Inland Revenue and old Social Security offices can be seen behind the City Library and Museum roof. The Maylord Orchards development is visible behind the cathedral tower and the cattle market behind All Saints Church spire. This wide angle view also shows the layout of the College Green estate. The photograph was taken from a helicopter supplied by Mike Davies Air Services of Hereford.

This postcard is of an unidentified bishop, possibly Bishop Percival, in the Palace gardens with his pigeons. The Cathedral site has had a church for over 1300 years but there are no remains of the first building which was built of timber. The Bishops Palace site may have a similar history and could even have been the site of the Saxon Cathedral. The building behind the Bishop is the Palace which contains some very early timbers and has long been recognised as being one of the most important Norman secular buildings in England. According to a recent archaeological article by John Blair the great hall, in which many timbers survive, was like the contemporary tithe barns. The closest remaining parallel to Hereford is the hall of Oakham Castle built during the 1180's.

This photograph was taken during a meeting of the Rotary Club of the City of Hereford held on the Palace lawns. On this special occasion, President Ron Munden welcomed the Bishop of Hereford the Rt Rev John Oliver into the club as an honorary member.

Most pictures of Hereford are of buildings, events were rarely photographed. The photograph above was taken in Broad Street on April 29th 1937. It shows the demolition of three houses in front of the Cathedral after a fire swept through the buildings. To the left just off the photograph was a shop occupied by Mrs Hammonds, a ladies hairdresser. In the white fronted house lived Walter Pritchard with his family, while next door was David L. Ellis, a saddler. To the extreme right was H. K. Foster, a land agent. By May 20th all the buildings had gone.

This photograph was taken by the late Mr G. Lewin of the demolition in Broad Street of three houses in front of the Cathedral in 1937. This picture was taken as a family snapshot and is still of interest today. The Broad Street name sign remains on the ivy covered wall. In the distance there is a policeman on duty while the old Austin car and cyclist make their way towards the old bridge. Because of the demoliton the west front of the Cathedral is now visible from Broad Street. The buildings were pulled down by the generosity of Col. Haywood of Caradoc Court.

The 1991 City carnival organised by the Chamber of Trade and Commerce on its way along King Street. The loss of the houses has opened up a very fine view of the Cathedral from both Broad Street and King Street. The City now awaits proposals for the site of a building to house the Mappa Mundi and Chained Library. Herefordians hope that it will not be here.

A cattle fair was held periodically in Broad Street. This photograph dates from the 1880s and about 30 heads of cattle are seen in the foreground with many more in the far distance. In between is a line of some ten horse-drawn 'taxi' cabs. The road surface looks well manured and the pedestrians are all on the pavements. Note the clean stone-fronted Post Office on the right — it had been opened only a few years earlier. No doubt the Public Houses, Inns and Hotels nearby were very busy during the fair. This picture was published in the Centenary edition of the *Hereford Times* in 1932.

The time gap between these two photographs is over 100 years and a comparison shows that most early buildings are still there. The building to the left, Thorpe House, is the only visible new arrival. Cattle fairs in Broad Street ended before the turn of the century. Both photographs were taken at about the same time of the day.

The Post Office in Broad Street was opened on December 20th 1882 with the cost of the building and fitting at £5,614. This photograph was taken in 1905 when James Ilsley was Postmaster. The office was open from 7.00am to 10.00pm except Sundays when the hours were 7.00am to 10.00am and 5.00pm to 6.00pm with only one letter delivery which also applied to bank holidays. In 1904 the GPO placed a contract with the carriers Connellys in Commerial Road. This was "to supply a carriage of mails by road motor". It was a regular service between Hereford, Clyro and Glasbury on Sundays only when there were no trains to Hay. By 1906 passengers were being carried in the mail van with all the mail sacks on the roof. Here is a twin cylinder Wolseley, registration number CJ239, which had solid rubber tyres on its rear wheels. In the photograph are representatives from both Connellys and the GPO.

The Post Office remains unaltered except for the stamp machines and post box. The mail van is small and no longer carries passengers. It is collecting the mail on Saturday 14th September at 12.30pm closing time.

This is a postcard view of the United Counties Bank at 50–51 Broad Street taken about 1910 when Arthur Chapman was manager. By 1922 the bank was a Barclays branch with Charles Lomax as the manager. The building has a fine stone front to Broad Street. The date sign at the top of the front refers to the original bank which was the Birmingham, District and Counties Banking Co. Ltd.

This fine old building is now in an excellent state of repair. The roof has been rebuilt and the top fascia chimney and attic replaced with a poor replica. The features would be highlighted if the stonework was to be repainted using a different colour.

Opposite top: The commercial centre of Hereford has been in and near High Town since the early Saxon defences were abandoned and the new city wall built. The wide open area was for an open market place and it is thought that the original area covered not only High Town but the land between Commercial Street and Union Street. Most of this was built over, including High Town, Butchers Row with the Old House, Cooken Row in Commercial Street and the old Town Hall which was built on wooden columns and originally extended upwards for three floors above ground level. This photograph, kindly loaned by Mr Johns, is of an unidentified event, but provides a wealth of detail in every area. Its date would be about 1890.

Opposite bottom: The progress of the 20th century has not changed many of the buildings seen in this view of High Town. The city centre is a conservation area and the local council has strong powers to ensure that historical features are preserved. The main changes visible are the paving and pedestrianisation of the whole area. The large trees now partly obscure the view of the beautiful Old House. This photograph was taken from the first floor window of the Midland Bank.

During the late 1960's the conservation of old buildings was often requested by local authorities, when developers wanted to demolish everything. These photographs show how a part of one building was retained. In High Street, Marchants old shop front was a mixture of original 17th century and late 19th century timber work. In 1967 Littlewoods purchased Marchants shop next to their existing building with a view to demolishing it and building a new store on the site. The oldest part was put on wheels and moved into High Town for some months while the new store was built. The framework for the new store is seen on the one photograph with Greenlands shop to the left, while the other picture shows the old part parked in High Town. In 1915 Wil-

liam Collins described Marchant &
Matthews shop thus: "The part
nearest High Town is faked and
modern, but the five light oriel windows with bold brackets under the
massive molded sill together with
elaborate rope and tassel, date
from the Tudor period. It is a gem
of the first order — and how soon
it may make way to modern business we know not." He was almost
correct. Pevsner dates the building
to c.1600.

The design of the Littlewoods store
has very little to commend it, except
that it incorporates the best part of
the old timber building though not
in its original position. To the left
is part of the Marks & Spencer
building which is also of a design
not in keeping with its neighbours
in High Town.

Hereford has had a very long history of receiving Royal visitors. This photograph shows Queen Mary on a visit to Hereford in her car driving past large crowds into High Town in the late 1920's. The Old House is visible on the left and behind is the Scotch Wool and Hosiery stores. The large double fronted building is occupied by Augustus Edwards "The Furriers of the West". They had the second largest store in High Town and it looks as if they are undergoing some restoration. The signs show that the main builder was Wm. Bowers & Co. of Bath Street and the architects were Bettington & Son. Messrs. J. E. Hiles were installing the plumbing and heating while Pollards supplied the curved non-reflecting windows. The three Midland Red buses are of a late 1920's design. Photograph taken by Percy Pritchard ARPS.

This is a photograph which is very similar to the old picture but mature trees hide most of the view across High Town. It is now proposed to replace the shop windows in the background with a 'period' design. The old concrete blocks which originally paved the newly pedestrianised High Town have now been replaced with bricks.

The May fair is held on the streets of the city centre during the first week of May. This photograph was taken by Mr E. J. Paynter and was published in the *Hereford Times* on May 25th 1907. The main roundabout in the centre is the Grand Steeplechase Gallopers. The traction engine, though not of the usual showman's type, was used to pull the showmen's wagons from town to town and generated electricity. In the foreground are the sidestalls while the Old House dominates the scene. The rights to hold the fair were granted in an old city charter of April 5th 1690 by William and Mary which reads: "Grant a three days fair at Easter with the accompanying right of a court of pie powder".

This photograph was taken from the second floor window of Marks & Spencer. The view of the May fair is now not as attractive as it is in the old picture. Note that there are no side stalls in High Town.

Kelly's Directory for 1895 listed the occupants at 24 and 25 High Town as Albert Townsend, cutler and optician, and William Pearce, grocer. In 1922 No. 24 was occupied by Frank Stewart, watchmaker and 25, by George Mason, grocers. In 1913 the building was auctioned and described in the brochure as follows: Mr Townsend had been there 30 years and paid a rent of £86 p.a. for his shop built in 1881 of brick and slate, a frontage of 13 feet 9 inches, depth of 56 feet. There were five bedrooms, pantry, dining room, drawing room, with a kitchen in the basement. No. 25 High Town had a Bath stone front 27 feet wide and extended through to East Street 169 feet in depth. It produced a rent of £200 p.a. The dwelling house above had seven bedrooms, drawing room, kitchen, bathroom. There were extensive warehouses, store rooms, a buttery, a tea storage room and a coal house. A cottage stood on the East Street frontage with three bedrooms let to Mr Pearce at £15 p.a.

In the early 1970's George Mason was still in business. However by 1980 the International Grocers had expanded the business next door into Fredricks 'ladies tailors' old shop. Note the very plain, rather ugly shop windows, and the false windows on the old Fredricks shop.

Hereford had its first glimpse of the new W. H. Smith store late in 1989 when scaffolding was removed after very extensive demolition and re-building. However the old Bath stone front and timber framed building behind was restored. A first floor plaster ceiling is now visible from the ground sales floor. The store opened in March 1991. This restoration and re-creation may well be a national conservation award winner.

The cinema in Hereford has its origins in the late 1890's when there were many Bioscope shows held at the city's Fairs. In 1910 such shows were stopped since the halls used did not have a proper projection room to conform with the Cinematograph Act. In the 1930's the Odeon group decided to build a cinema in Hereford so in September 1936 the company — Odeon (Hereford) Ltd was registered. It was built on the site of the Judges Lodgings at 5 Commercial Street — cost £28,000, seated 1,133, and opened on 17th April 1937. The builders were Peake & Son of Hereford. The original Odeon sign was replaced by the 'Focus' name owned by Brent Walker group in 1975. In 1983 it was decided that the building would be demolished for development. 'Classic' took over the lease on 3rd June 1983 and closed on 1st March 1984 with the film *Trading Places* starring Dan Ackroyd. Demolition took place in 1985. The Odeon clock is on public view in the museum on the staircase. On the right of the Odeon is a substantial Georgian period house and shops, one of which is occupied by Mr Latif, the other recently vacated by a carpet company. The photograph was taken just prior to demolition. Note the bus sign — this is where the Nation's first private bus companies were allowed to compete against the national carriers. References were taken from *90 Years of the Cinema in Hereford* by Brian Hornsby to whom the author is grateful.

Old Herefordians returning to the city notice the loss of the old Odeon cinema but now it is no longer clear where it once stood. The new Maylord Orchards development does blend into the old buildings and with time the newly-built look will weather away.

The Old House, High Town, Hereford.

Old air photographs of Hereford are quite rare. This picture postcard is of High Town and part of Commercial Street (to the lower right corner). The Old House is clearly visible near the centre lower edge with All Saints church and spire to the top. Visible features are the long roof of the Butter Market with Maylord Street to the centre right. Just above the name Hereford is the Odeon cinema auditorium. Older Herefordians will remember the Brewery in Bewell Street as well as the British Canners nearby. Other features to look for are the *Hereford Times* building in Maylord Street, Greenlands in High Town, the small Midland Bank, and the caravans in Gomond Street. The buildings in Newmarket Street and the old cattle market can also be seen.

Today the same view but with a wide angle lens clearly shows many major changes in the city centre. Greenlands have made way for a new Marks & Spencer building. The Odeon site has become part of the Maylord Orchards centre, The Brewery and British Canners are Tesco's and Red Lion corner is now a block of flats. This photograph was taken from a helicopter supplied by Mike Davies of M. D. Air Services, Bullingham, Hereford.

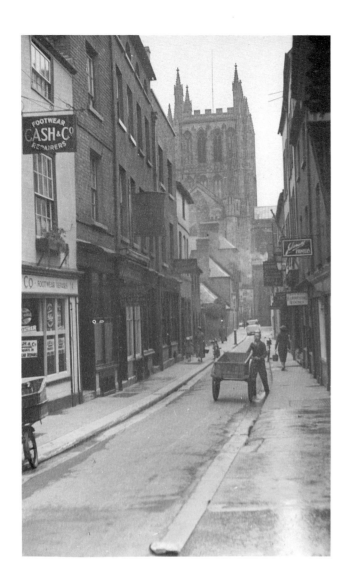

This postcard view of Church Street was taken about 1935. The Cathedral is the focal point of the picture and in the far distance is a motor car while in the foreground is a delivery bicycle and a handcart. The street, which is one of the oldest in the city, has had many names — in 1220 it was known as Caboge Lane, in 1397 Cabache Lane, in 1757 Capuchin or Cabbage Lane and by 1833 had become Church Street. To the left are 'Cash & Co Footwear Repairers' where in 1905 the owner was Thomas Vale, bootmaker, then during the 1920's the shop was occupied by W. E. Turner, also a bootmaker. The next shop was Mrs Everett, a poulterer and the sign above the Cathedral Cafe which is just legible, reads 'Bed and Breakfast'. The far sign is Madame Raymond who sold costumes. The signs to the right of the street read: 'Stevens Antiques', 'Williams Hairdresser', 'Jakemans Ltd.' (printers and bookbinders).

The street was one of the first to be pedestrianised in the city being paved from wall to wall eliminating curbs. The shop on the left is now S. G. Skinner, 'High Class Footwear Repairs' who no longer have the small shop window panes. The other businesses are a wool shop, camera shop (now closed), Vivians Studio, Cafe, hairdresser and a recently opened nature shop. The shops on the right include a bookshop, kitchenware, crafts, antiques, natural health foods, a craft yard and a jeweller. Today the corner of the Cathedral tower is undergoing repairs and has been encased in scaffolding for about 18 months. Works are expected to be completed soon.

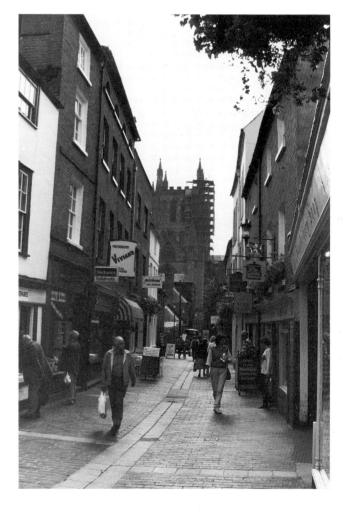

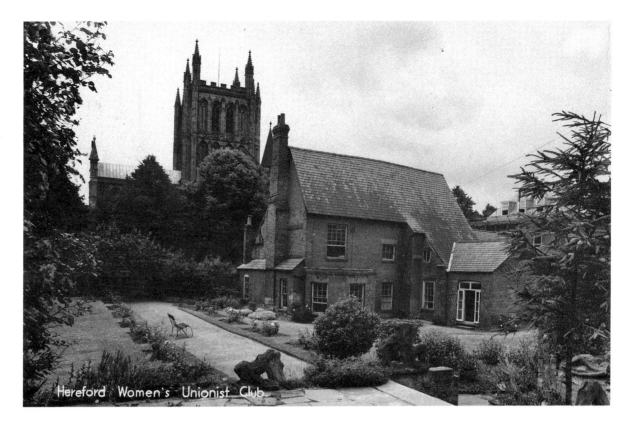

Hereford Women's Unionist Club

Here is a peaceful retreat in the city centre. It is the garden and house at 20 Church Street where Sir Edward Elgar was a frequent visitor. The building, which is not seen from Church Street, was once occupied by the Cathedral organist G. R. Sinclair. His dog Dan was featured in Elgar's Enigma Variations and Dan's gravestone survives in the garden. In a recent survey of the structure, City Archaeologist Ron Shoesmith and his team reported that it was originally a 14th century hall with a crown post roof. He also suggests that other than the Bishops Palace this is the only building to survive of the several ecclesiastical residences which surrounded the Cathedral at that time.

The cottage has just had an extension built on the north side while the old part is undergoing extensive repairs. When restored there will be an 'Elgar' room open to the public. In the gardens are many stones removed from the Cathedral during earlier restorations.

At the turn of the century there were 17 hairdressers in Hereford. Most were to be found along the main commercial streets. This photograph of Langfords salon was taken in West Street which was behind Greenlands shop. In 1895 the salon was owned by Henry Powell and by 1905 Ernest Langford was the new proprietor. In 1914 William Williams was recorded as owning the business and was still there in 1937. He was known as 'General' Williams. Please refer to *Hereford Then and Now* published 1988 page 35 where the salon can be seen in the distance along West Street.

In 1968 Littlewoods demolished all the buildings along the West Street front and built their new store. This area is now used for unloading delivery vehicles and is not picturesque. This photograph is of Mrs Sheila Hughson, Mr Langford's grand-daughter, who visited the site of the old salon in September 1991.

Opposite top: This photographic postcard was taken in front of Hereford Cathedral in 1933 during the Three Choirs Festival. It shows four very famous people. They are, standing from the left — the Cathedral organists Sir Ivor Atkins (Worcester), Sir Percy Hull (Hereford), Sir H. W. Sumsion (Gloucester) and seated is Sir Edward Elgar who was 76 years of age. He lived in Hereford between 1904 and 1911 at Plas Gwynne, Hampton Park Road. Here he composed some of his most famous works including the *Allegro for strings*, the *Violin Concerto*, *The Kingdom*, *The Dream of Gerontius* and the *Cello Concerto*. Some weeks after this photograph was taken, it was found that a malignant tumour in his spine was causing sciatica. Five months after the festival he died. To this day his works are still performed at every festival.

Opposite bottom The 1991 Three Choirs Festival was held in Hereford. In the photograph are the three Cathedrals' organists, from the left: Dr Donald Hunt, Worcester Cathedral; Dr Roy Massey, Hereford Cathedral; and Dr John Saunders, Gloucester Cathedral. Seated is composer Dr John Joubert whose works have been heard during this and previous years' festivals.

Following the end of the Great War the city honoured its dead by erecting a temporary wooden cenotaph in High Town. This postcard shows the first service at the new stone memorial in St Peter's Square which was unveiled on 7th October 1922 by Lieut. Colonel Gilbert Drage DSO, and Colonel M. J. Scobie CB of the Herefordshire Regiment. They committed the memorial to the safekeeping of the Corporation. The memorial is in the shape of an eleanor cross, octagonal in plan inscribed to the men of Herefordshire who fell in the Great War 1914–1919. It is 30 feet 3 inches in height and made from Darley Dale quarried stone with steps of Cotswold stone and figures in Portland stone. It was designed by Mr L. W. Barnard FRIBA of Cheltenham.

This photograph was taken on April 9th 1989 during the re-dedication of the War Memorial. Present were armed forces detachments, which included a representation from the city's adopted submarine HMS *Warspite*, and a band. The mayor Basil Baldwin and the Lord Lieutenant Col. Thomas Dunne were in attendance. The dedication was conducted by the late Bishop Rt Rev. John Eastaugh and wreaths were laid.

The city has been very fortunate in having several bands for very many years, including those of the TA, and Salvation Army. Here is the Salvation Army band at the front of the Shirehall before a performance. The Salvation Army was founded in 1882 by General William Booth (who visited Hereford in 1911) and founder members were reported to have suffered riot, bloodshed and imprisonment. Early barracks were in an old wooden warehouse in Widemarsh Street. New buildings were obtained in Maylord Street in 1911 which have been extended and re-built over the years, the last being in 1963.

The old Citadel was demolished in 1986 to make way for the Maylord Orchards centre. A new site was found in Edgar Street, and a new Citadel built which has received awards for its excellent design. The Hereford Citadel Band originated with the foundation of the Army in Hereford. In 100 years it has had only seven bandmasters. In September 1991 the Salvation Army Band kindly assembled for a re-enactment of the 1931 photograph. The uniform has changed, so have their numbers but not their enthusiasm and quality of music. The bandmaster Ken Farr is on the front row fourth from the left. The Shirehall is undergoing extensive repairs so the exact position could not be used. Note the renovated columns to the left.

Opposite: During the mid-Victorian times and earlier the city civic offices were in the old Town Hall which stood on 27 wood pillars in High Town. This was demolished in 1862. However as early as 1809 the Council bought land and two Inns — The Red Streak in Maylord Street and New Inn, Widemarsh Street. The New Inn was partly converted into a council chamber. In 1882 the Mansion House (presently Blacks shop, Widemarsh Street) was leased from Sam Farmer for 14 years with rent at £120 p.a.

The new Town Hall in St Owen Street was opened in 1904 by Princess Henry of Battenberg. It is built in terracotta and brick in the Renaissance style from designs of architect Mr H. A. Cheers from Twickenham. It cost £25,000 to build and was erected by Messrs Williams Bowers & Co. of Bath Street. In 1914 it was described as having various municipal offices and being used for public meetings etc. The photograph on the left, kindly loaned by Mrs Smith, shows William Bowers standing in the foreground, with all his 34 workmen and supervisors behind and above. Note the two men on the ridge tiles. This picture was taken in 1904.

During 1980 the Town Hall was renovated and the photograph above is an interesting comparison. The old wooden scaffolding was in places bundled together in lengths of three poles, where today a single tube is used no matter how high the building.

Here is a photograph which was originally owned by the late Ray Bubb — motorcycle engineer of Cross Street. It shows his uncle, who was also a motorcycle engineer, in 1903 outside his shop in St Owen Street. His name was Sydney Thomas Owen and worked in his 'namesake' street. Mr Owen is seen standing in the doorway with some of his work outside on the pavement. Note the wicker seated trailer which would be attached to a motorcycle seat pillar. The motorcycle behind the seat is a 1903 Minerva which was one of the earliest reliable motorcycles, and made in Belgium. The motorcycle on the right side of the shop has had its engine removed for repair. The tricycle in the middle seems to be one of Mr Owen's inventions. There is a penny farthing cycle mounted on the wall above the entrance. Vales shoe repair shop window is just visible on the left.

The old buildings have been de-molished and the present ones built about 1955. The charity shop is one of many to be found in the city.

The photographer has recorded a quiet view of the junction of the Ledbury Road and St Owen Street. It shows the St Giles Hospital Almshouses on the left with the St Giles Chapel protruding out onto the pavement. In 1914 St Giles Hospital was described as being for five poor men. It was believed to have been founded in 1290 for Friars Grisey or Savignian monks but now this information is thought to be incorrect. Later it became the property of the Knights Templars and being seized by the Crown was given by Richard II to the city and appropriated to the purpose of an almshouse. In 1682 it was rebuilt as an almshouse using voluntary subscriptions. There are five houses, each with a piece of land. The Chapel of St Giles with an inscription above the door states that it was rebuilt from the ground and out of the ruins of the previous building by Richard Cox, Custos. of the College of Vicars AD 1682. Out of sight to the left of the photograph is the Williams Hospital rebuilt in 1892 at a cost of £300.

In 1927 the chapel was demolished for widening the adjacent road junction of Ledbury Road and St Owen Street. During this process the foundation of the early building was found. It was of a round shape 27 feet in diameter, with a domed roof and attached chancel of the Norman period. Speed's map of 1610 indicates that it was standing then. Alfred Watkins discovered that it stood on a ley line. In 1928 a brass plate was put on the new wall on the site which read: "The stones below were part of the walls of the twelfth century round chapel of St Giles found in 1927 when demolishing the chapel of 1682." Today the chapel is re-built and stands next to Williams Hospital. It is used for a service once a week on a Monday afternoon.

CIRCA 1917

Opposite: Here are two photographs which are on public display inside the building in St Owen Street. The oldest, a blurred but interesting view shows No. 74 St Owen Street about 1917 when it was a chapel. In a 1895 directory it was listed as the 'Salvation Army Barracks'. The second picture taken about 1925 shows a change of use to a cinema called 'The Pavilion'. Cinema historian Brian Hornsby in his book *90 Years of Cinema in Hereford* records that between June 1919 and 1923 it was called The Kinema and seated 368 people, had a music licence and changed its programme three times a week. The music for the silent films was provided by a lady pianist. The name changed in 1924 to 'The Pavilion' but was closed in 1926 when the building was sold. In 1929 it was occupied by 'The Co-operative Industrial Society'. Note that the windows have been bricked up for the cinema and the gas lamps removed. The photograph is of an outing to the cinema by charabanc.

The building remained a branch of the Hereford Co-operative Society from 1929 until comparatively recently when the building was sold and turned into a launderette. The old Co-op shop front has been retained and this is one cinema that has not been converted into a Bingo hall.

In 1895 this building in Bath Street was described as the 'Industrial Aid Society's Flour Mills' where William Lloyd was secretary and manager. An invoice for 1902 advertised that they sold flour in free sacks weighing from 140lbs to 280lbs. Sacks with meal or offal cost 6d. each and were not returnable unless pre-purchased. All feedstuffs were described as not pure since they were prepared from more than one substance or seed. The engraving on the invoice showed the mills with a huge chimney for the steam engine which powered the machinery. Water was extracted from a nearby bore hole. Note the grain hoist protruding from the middle of the building. The Society for Aiding the Industrious was founded by the vicar of St Peters, the Rev John Venn who helped the poor by letting allotments of land on ground near Bath Street, opening a soup kitchen in severe weather, by lending sums of between £1 and £15 at a very low interest, providing baths amply supplied with hot water and by opening up a large swimming pool in November 1871 in Kyrle Street.

The distant cottages were demolished to make way for a car park. Those near the camera were replaced initially by a carpenter's workshop owned by Mr Jelfs who lived in one of the cottages, and later by an office extension and car park. Note the loss of the protruding hoist box on the front of the building which is at present used as a business centre. Bath Street was widened as a part of the inner relief road some 20 years ago.

When found, this old picture postcard had no identification on it except that the donor knew it was supposed to be of Hereford. However after a lot of research and walking, the author realised that he walked past the site every day! It is of the junction of Kyrle Street (just visible between the houses) and Bath Street. The picture would date about 1935 or earlier. In the cottage near the camera was Albert Jelfs a cabinet maker, with William Owen from the Hereford City Mission next door. The house seen behind the lamp post is Florida House occupied by a Mrs Hirons. Note the profusion of chimneys.

This wide angle view identifies the area in front of the Police Station. The cottages have been demolished and there is now a car park. Several of the distant houses are used as offices.

The city of Hereford Police Force used to own many houses. Here is a 'family snapshot' of De Lacy Street taken from Bath Street. The city police station is hidden from view behind the row of terraced houses. The old city gaol once stood here. It was built in 1842 and closed in 1877 when the corporation re-purchased it for £1,750. One wing was then used as the city police station. Another converted into a fire engine house, while other parts were demolished to make way for a new street between Gaol Street and Bath Street-De Lacy Street. In 1884 the corporation built a terraced row of cottages on either side for £12,200 to be used as barracks for the police. The low building on the right side was built as a soup kitchen annex to the offices of the Hereford Society for the Industrious founded by the Rev John Venn.

The whole of De Lacy Street was demolished to make way for a new police station which is a very plain and uninspiring design. There are plans to build an enquiry office and reception area on the ground level behind the columns. The remains of the city wall are visible behind the bench seat. The building was opened by Tom Barnes, Chairman of the West Mercia Police Authority, on 6th April 1976.

Here is a view of the north side of Commercial Street taken by architect Mr Bettington in 1914, just before the demolition of the three closed shops near the lamp post. The middle building with the tall chimney stack was a stationers owned by Mr Henry Brewer. The large sign on the shop which reads 'Your King and Country need you' — a famous recruiting slogan for the first World War — is on Lindsey-Price's new shop.

The 'new' building has a date stone 1915 and is named 'Wilsons Chambers'. Family descendants still run the florists and garden centre shop. The narrow building with 'bow' windows remains with the author's business on the upper floors. The building with columns was originally Lindsey Price, but is now occupied by the Halifax Building Society. The street has become a thriving pedestrian area which was paved two years ago.

Opposite top: The Three Choirs Festival is held in Hereford once every three years. Here is a very busy Commercial Street and several workmen are erecting a very elaborate festival arch across the road. In the background is another decorative arch. The near arch has an Egyptian theme with an inscription banner which reads 'The Three Choirs — long may their union continue'. The shop on the side is a grocers owned by C. W. Slatter. Next door is William Harris a clothier. Mr Corner's hardware shop is clearly visible with his painted sign: Gas, Water and Fittings. The date is not known but would be before 1910. Note the man half way up the ladder with some decorative branches. The famous copper kettle can be seen below the Union flag.

Commercial Street was closed to traffic three years ago and then paved. A comparison with the old photograph does show the considerable number of new buildings. Only the building on the far side of Halfords remains unchanged. A fire on the evening of Thursday December 8th 1983 destroyed Goldings shop (*opposite bottom*). The copper kettle survived and is now seen on the new Halfords shop.

J. COATES & SON,
Watch and Clock Makers, Jewellers, and Opticians,
49, COMMERCIAL STREET, HEREFORD.
SPECIAL ATTENTION GIVEN TO REPAIRS.

At the turn of the century Hereford had a large number of watch and clock makers, jewellers and opticians. The area had an affluent population and it seems that most jewellers survived for many years. All were small family businesses and there were no national chains of shops. Here we see Mr Coates of 49 Commercial Street who advertised that he was not only a jeweller and clock maker but an optician as well. His window has samples of all his stock on show which includes a large selection of watches and gold chains. During the 1870's the upper floors were used as offices by the Society for Aiding the Industrious founded by the Rev John Venn.

The modern shop front is virtually all glass which gives a good view into the shop. It is interesting to see the old tradition of displaying goods on the pavement — but for self service. The old Coates sign bracket fixing between the upper windows can still be seen.

During the early years of the century Hereford had only two shops which were part of a national chain. All the rest were mainly either a single family shop, or one of just a few branches. This is a picture of William Price the newsagent in Commercial Street, with his three assistants. The bicycle looks new and may be the delivery bike. The newsboard advertises the *Daily Mail* and the *Daily Express*. In the left window can be seen jewellery, handkerchiefs and clothes while on the right are pipes, tobacco and accessories. The wall sign advertises MacDonalds teeth, while the door leads upstairs to the dentist. The three substantial gas lamps illuminate the window display as well as the pavement.

This building which is now restored, has a first floor office and a second floor flat which is half timbered. The ground floor shop to the left has been used as a charity shop while to the right is the Matabeau Cafe with the owner's wife Mrs Teresa Moruzzi outside.

Opposite: Queen Victoria's Diamond Jubilee was celebrated nationally and in the colonies. This 1897 photograph of Commercial Street shows Mr Christopher Vaughan and staff outside his shop which has been well dressed for the occasion. All the men are wearing their Sunday best suits and hats. Mr Vaughan was a builder and sanitary engineer. Next door, to the left, can be seen Vaughan & Co. Steam Laundry. By 1905 the laundry had gone and the Hereford Conservative Association were the occupiers. If this photograph had been in colour it would have been a brilliant display of flags, drapes, foliage and shields. Note the stone arches on the ground floor level with Vaughan's name seen on the arch above the small boy.

A close inspection of the photograph does show how extensive the alterations have been. The roof has been completely rebuilt as well as the windows. The present owners Chadds have made an effort to return the shop windows to a more period design in keeping with its range of ancient buildings the oldest part of which dates back to about 1540.

W. H. Smith has had a long history in Hereford. Their first retail outlet was a bookstall at the railway station in the late Victorian period. In 1906 they opened their first shop in Stonebow House, Commercial Road which later became Hartford Motors. This was closed in 1909 when they purchased No. 46 Commercial Street. This photograph, kindly supplied by the company archivist Mr Baker Jones, is of the Commercial Street shop about 1922. The window display on the left has a selection of greetings cards while that on the right is of a wide selection of books. The side entrance leads upstairs to the Wye River Board where Major F. A. Phillips DSO was the Clerk. This shop front remained until 1975 when the side entrance was removed and a full width front fitted.

The old W. H. Smith shop closed in the spring of 1991 and the firm moved to their new shop in High Town (see page 21). The building has recently been purchased by Chadds of Hereford and will open for the 1991 Christmas sales. Next year (1992) it will be renovated and incorporated into its department store next door.

The street sign on the building reads Commercial Road. The house is one of three Temperance Hotels listed along Commercial Road at the turn of the century and was called 'Farmers'. The hotel front is a Georgian design with interesting stonework above the windows. Note the hanging gas lamp above the front door and Mr Rodgers the owner below. Next door is Franklin Barnes shop, who were seed and corn merchants. The corner on the extreme left leads into Blueschool Street. By 1929 the hotel had been converted into shops. The first was the Sanitary Laundry, where they had their receiving office. Next door was the Hereford Wallpaper Co. and then Mr H. S. Marchant the tobacconist. Upstairs was Mr Joseph Hiles a dentist. In an advert dated 1914 Mr Hiles proclaimed that he had been an assitant to Mr Edgar Billing and Mr Gerald Thompson for 29 years. The author, a dentist, wonders whether he was a slow learner! Franklin Barnes were still in the same shop, but advertised that their head office was in 13 Bridge Street with the sample office at 34 Broad Street and the retail branch in 4 Commercial Road.

Most of the site where the old building was is now incorporated into the widened inner relief road and the new Franklin Barnes House has become a well established landmark. The road junction is now one of the busiest in the city.

The Herefordshire and South Wales Eye and Ear Institution was established in Commercial Road on July 1st 1882 by the Hon Surgeon Mr F. W. Lindsay with funds raised by a few private subscribers. The need for such an institution was fully demonstrated by the work load it had to bear and opened on January 1st 1884 as a public Institution. The building soon proved to be too small and unsuitable. In Queen Victoria's Jubilee year 1897 funds were raised to build a more suitable hospital which opened on 20th August 1889 along Eign Street. This photograph, of the Institution in Commercial Road was taken about 1890. The Baptist Church is just visible on the left side of the photograph and there are steps between the pavement level and the road surface.

If Herefordians wondered why the Baptist Church was built some distance away from the road here is the answer. The loss of the old hospital (before 1905) has opened up the full frontage of the church to Commercial Road.

During the last years of the Victorian era the buildings seen in this photograph were from left to right: a bakers, grocers, and Temperance hotel run by James Davis. Just after the last war the whole block was purchased by H. A. Saunders. They opened their garage and called it Austin House. Note the petrol pump under the archway which was the entrance to the workshop at the rear of the building. There are six cars visible in the showroom which advertised they also sold car radios. There are many local people who would have purchased a car here.

The archway, petrol pumps and advertising signs have gone leaving a plain but tidy area. The old workshops at the rear of the building are now used for the sale of furniture and carpets. H. A. Saunders took over Thornes of Worcester and they in turn were bought by Mann Egerton who closed down about 10 years ago.

In very recent years some parts of the city have undergone very considerable changes. This photograph shows a collection of buildings last used as an engineering works with the part adjacent to Commercial Road used as a temporary furniture shop. On the corner of Station Approach and Commercial Road was a small public toilet. The large building was erected at the turn of the century by coach builders Connellys. They arrived in Hereford from Ireland in late Victorian times and had works in Union Street and Ross Road before their move into Commercial Road. Here they made all types of horse drawn vehicles from dog carts to carriages for transporting judges to court. They provided a significant part of the early horse drawn public transport in the city as well as a service from the Railway Station nearby. In 1908 they introduced a motorbus into the city. This site was listed in 1905 as having wool merchants, an architectural sculptor and the Stroud Brewery.

Three years ago when the whole site was demolished the city archaeology unit carried out some excavations near the old Monkmoor Mill where some remains were found. The new Safeways and carpark does at least give a tidy appearance to the area.

The treatment of disease with herbs is said to be as old as mankind itself. The Ancient Egyptians, the Romans and Indians made extensive use of plants for healing and today the Chinese and Indians continue to do so. In Britain from the Dark Ages to well into Medieval times herbal remedies were copied by hand in monasteries. In London, in 1812, Henry Potter established his shop selling herbs and leeches and his cyclopaedia is still published. The World Health Organisation estimates that today herbalism is four times more commonly used than conventional medicine of which 15% of prescriptions are plant based. This photograph taken about 1920 is of Mr W. Pigott outside his shop in Commercial Road. It was the only one in the county and continued in business until 1960 when he died., He was a local character, well liked and served on the City Council for many years. He was made Alderman in 1947 and Mayor in 1949. The window sign reads 'Herbs positively cure diseases'.

The upper windows have been replaced and the ground floor shop has been enlarged by expanding into the left hand unit. The shop front is of a plain, unimaginative design not in keeping with the building.

The date of this 'double' or panoramic photograph is 1937 and was taken at the 'new' bus station. It is on the site of the old Prison where in 1895 Joseph Flockton was chief warder and acting Prison Governor. In 1935 a Miss Skyrme was living in the Prison Officers house. The old gaol was demolished in 1935 when local people were invited to inspect the buildings on payment of 6d. before the contractors moved in. In 1927 bus services were centralised in St Peter's Square with the shelters paid for by the Birmingham Midland Omnibus Co. Not unexpectedly the vicar of St. Peter's Church was quite vociferous about this and suggested a proper station. Soon after the disused gaol in Commercial Road was purchased by the city after prolonged negotiations. It was very spacious and the frontage to Commercial Road was reserved for a cinema, café and shops. The former Governor's house was preserved and converted into a waiting room and enquiry offices for two major companies. A small garage for six buses was built behind. The City Council charged a rent of one penny for each departure to recoup costs. It is of interest to note that Yeomans Motors had one complete platform out of the five at a rent of £25 p.a. and the Midland Red had two platforms for £100. From here buses served 18 different routes. The buses shown with HA registration numbers are from Birmingham. The bus second from the left was made by S.O.S. and operated during the war years. The office is on the right.

This building has recently been fully renovated. The cast iron shelter was built just before the war and the cinema on the left was opened on 10th January 1938. The angle of the bus lanes has been altered and the old prison wall has been lowered.

Opposite: Herefordians will remember this sight along Commercial Road. All the buildings were worth restoring but it was not to be. All were built during the early 1800's and had a new roof put on in 1982. This photograph was taken by Graham Wrightson an architect with John Brunton Partnership from Bradford, just before demolition in 1990. A street directory of 1895 listed Mrs Amelia Plant as the owner with apartments at No. 32. Next door on her right at No. 33 was Felix Ford, a fruit merchant and at No. 34 was John Holloway.

The terraced row of houses though worthy and suitable for restoration would have kept the character of the road, but unfortunately were demolished early in 1990. Soon a very ugly steel framework was erected and it was obvious that something special was going on. Large blocks of dressed stone arrived and a frontage of brick and stone went up. Today the completed offices show that the architect had made an effort though some say that the result is more suited to a London Mayfair site. However this has done no harm to the appearance of the city and is now something of a landmark. Barclays Bank have a managerial suite of offices and business centre on the ground and first floors. Integrated Security Systems Ltd. are on the second floor.

Early photographs taken inside Hereford Railway Station are very rare. This was taken by Mr Zimmerman early this century on the north bound platform. The Station was opened at the same time as the railway to Shrewsbury on December 6th 1853 which was the first into Hereford and was called the Shrewsbury and Hereford Railway. The very well dressed ladies are just about to board the first class carriage at the platform. Photograph kindly loaned by Basil Butcher.

This photograph was taken on Sunday 5th May 1991 at the Hereford Rail Festival which was the first and last held in the freight yard. Seen in the locomotive is the Dean of Hereford the Very Rev Peter Haines who had just finished a dedication service and then named the locomotive *Mappa Mundi*. He said the name stood for pilgrimage, travel and movement.

Assembly in Yard, Blue Coat School, Hereford

The Bluecoat School was in Blueschool Street — a narrow road connecting Widemarsh Street to Commercial Square. In late Victorian times there were wheelwrights, a shoemaker, dressmakers, a plumber, tailor, wool merchants, blacksmith, bill poster etc. in the street. The School, which was established in 1710 in St Peters parish, is a red brick building with stone corners and window apertures. In 1910 it was partly rebuilt to accommodate the 450 children, 250 boys and 200 girls with an average attendance of 358. This photograph, taken about 1920 when the headmaster was William Caldwell, shows the boys on playground parade. The playground is on the Coningsby Street side of the School, where the entrance was.

The buildings remain intact, but the school closed some ten years ago. Today it is used as a small factory manufacturing windows. Here is Mr Teague a director of the family firm.

This is M. Black's shop in Widemarsh Street photographed by Jean O'Donnell in 1968 prior to the construction of the inner ring road. The Old Harp Inn is seen behind the shop where in 1895 George Pearman was landlord. The building which is just visible on the extreme right was a butchers on the corner of Blueschool Street and Widemarsh Street. M. Black's shop — a general drapers and outfitters, was an attractive timber framed building with a rendered front. It was demolished to make way for the inner ring road in 1968 — a very sad loss to the city.

The Old Harp remains and M. Black's business has relocated to another ancient and interesting building — the Mansion House in Widemarsh Street. Hereford lost an important timber framed building which today may well have been rebuilt elsewhere.

Some parts of the city were rarely photographed and no photographs have been found of the Garrick Theatre. This *Hereford Times* picture of Widemarsh Street dates from about 1968. The photograph which will bring back many memories to Herefordians does show the arched windows and doors which were the old theatre front. Here, it was used as a County Library and early Records Office for the post war years. Inside the floors were creaky and uneven. Brian Hornsby reports that the Garrick Theatre lost is cinematographic licence to the new Ritz when it opened in 1938 on the site of the old gaol. This virtually closed the Garrick. In 1895 the occupants of the shop on the left were J. & R. Millar, drapers. The theatre was the Athenaeum with Edward Shenton, lessee, while the building on the right, the George Inn was run by Julia Watkins. The theatre name changed about the turn of the century to the Garrick Theatre. In 1915 the theatre was the property of the Hereford Lodge of the Oddfellows which was licenced for theatrical performances and cinematographic shows.

The new building is a multi-storey car park of a pleasing design which is a useful asset to the city for residents and visitors alike. Only a small part of the old theatre remains — a carved balcony panel which can be seen in the New Hereford Theatre auditorium.

Turnpike gates were established in 1663 at which tolls were taken from passengers in vehicles to pay for the upkeep of the roads. The county turnpikes were abolished later than those in the city. The Local Government Act of 1888 put the entire maintenance of main roads on the county councils. The city had turnpike gates at Aylestone Hill, St Owens, Above Eign, Widemarsh and St Martins. They were all abolished in 1870. This photograph is of the Widemarsh Gate. The building on the left is the Essex Arms — occupied by Mrs Sophie Parry. In the background on the right side of the road at 75–78 was Symonds Hospital founded in 1695 for four persons.

The central road markings pass over the site of the old pedestrian gate. There is no identification left to show the exact position of the old gate. The Essex Arms was removed and re-built (right) at considerable expense, on Dinmore Hill as a café. Though now preserved in a beautiful environment this building was a loss to the city.

This is an unposted photographic postcard which was not identified. It was thought to be a house in Hereford and after a long search the author found it to be in Elm Road. The house name, *Windermere, 1898* is engraved on the wall plaque seen above the front entrance. Note the dog behind the gate.

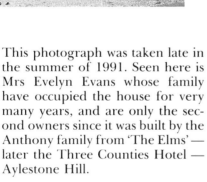

This photograph was taken late in the summer of 1991. Seen here is Mrs Evelyn Evans whose family have occupied the house for very many years, and are only the second owners since it was built by the Anthony family from 'The Elms' — later the Three Counties Hotel — Aylestone Hill.

Opposite top: In the late 1920's when ice cream was sold from a 'stop me and buy one' pedal tricycle this photograph shows how King's were ahead of the times. The picture was taken in Coningsby Street with the Boys High School in the background. The van is an attractive conversion of a 1926 Austin Seven which has a Hereford motor registration number. The roof level has been raised but only enough to allow a person of five feet or less to stand inside. William King had his confectionery corner shop at No. 98 Widemarsh Street adjacent to Coningsby Street. Many ex-pupils from the high schools will remember Mr King and his daughter who carried on business from 1924 up to recent years.

Opposite below: The popularity of the mobile ice cream van has not declined and today many tour the city estates during the summer months. Here Roy Raithatha of the Hereford Ice Cream Co. kindly re-enacted the scene. The old school buildings are now a Teachers Education Centre and a Technical and Vocational centre.

At the turn of the century Venns Lane had five large houses and several cottages. This photograph was taken in 1898 outside 'Elmhurst' which is at the junction of Aylestone Hill and Venns Lane. In 1892 estate agent F. H. Merrick advertised 'Elmhurst' as having the following: entrance hall, breakfast room, dining room, drawing room, library, servants hall, butlers pantry, kitchen, seven bedrooms, bathroom, WC and four cellars. There were attached stables, coach and cow house with loft over. The gardens and grounds extended to over 10 acres. In 1898 Elmhurst was owned by the Boulton family who also owned Barrs Court Cider Stores in Rockfield Road where they had a cider factory. The small boy on the pony is the son, who many years later presented Elmhurst with a set of photographs of the house including this picture. The carriage, horses and footman/driver no doubt made all the utility trips into Hereford, while the family used a carriage with weather protection.

The local authority who own and run the house as a residential home for the elderly have just fully renovated the whole of the building. Note the loss of the castellated top along the wall.

This photograph is one of a series of 'Elmhurst' taken by Bustin in 1898. The picture was taken in the music room with the piano keyboard visible on the left. To the right, the marble and stone fireplace can be seen. The photographer's camera was against the french windows which open into the garden, while at the far end of the room are the open staircase and hall, so the music would be heard throughout the house. Note the marble and wood columns and arch mouldings at the far end — also the two wall mounted gas lamps.

Most of the original features have been retained in the restoration and a fire screen wall has been inserted between the arches at the end of the room, separating the inner entrance hall and staircase from the residents lounge.

Until the early 1950s much of the city area of Holmer parish was farmland, with a few cottages and a farm — The Crossway. The farm boundary was along the Holmer Road, Roman Road, Old School Lane and the City Gasworks. Henry Wiggin, who were already situated in Glasgow and Birmingham, decided to expand and relocate to Hereford in 1952. This photograph from the company archives was taken in 1953 and shows construction of the main factory area from the site entrance on Holmer Road. The buildings seen in the distance included a melting shop and huge extrusion press. To the left are the offices, laboratory and medical centre. The Crossway Farm, when sold in 1919, was described as having 65 acres with a superior and detached farmhouse, a bailiff's house, and workmen's cottage. It was in the occupancy of Mr Creswell who paid a rent of £195p.a. It was sold for £6,600 to the tenant.

Since the main factory opened for production in 1954 the company have extended over the area to the right, along Holmer Road, along the Roman Road and across Old School Lane. In recent years the buildings along the Holmer Road have been sold and now their use includes the Hereford Times offices, a small industrial estate and two main car dealer garages.

ILY MAIL AEROPLANE AT HEREFORD. F.PREECE PHOTO

During the pre-first world war days an aeroplane was a very rare sight in the county. The pioneer aviators were very brave and there were no purpose built airfields. This photograph shows Mr M. Salmet 'The Daily Mail Flying Man' at the Hereford city racecourse on Friday 26th July 1912. He took off from Cardiff on July 20th and arrived at Raglan to refuel. Misty weather prevented him leaving for Hereford on that day, so he motored to Ross-on-Wye to stay at an hotel. A reception committee was planned to await his arrival at Hereford but this had to be disbanded because of the delay. However, on the 26th he duly arrived, having flown at 5,000ft. and was met at 5.00pm by S. H. Armitage the secretary of the racecourse. The reception committee consisted of Mr H. P. Bulmer, Mr Frank Greenland and Mr E. Hatton. The arrival of the aeroplane was described as resembling a huge dragonfly and the reception as the best ever. This photograph shows the Blériot aeroplane and its 50 hp Gnome engine. Note how the machine is held together with thin wires. The city grandstand is visible in the background.

Until about 1950 the racecourse ran across the Holmer Road before it was moved to the west where it could be completely self-contained. Today, the area houses sports facilities for the city which include a leisure centre, all weather running track, sports field and golf course. The old grandstand remains and is now used by the City Sports Club. A new grandstand has been built on the north side of the racecourse. Aeroplanes have not landed here for over 40 years.

Clarence House is near the corner of Edgar Street and Portland Street. In 1895 James Mitchell, a tailor, was the occcupant of 12 and 13 Edgar Street, ie the whole of the large house, while William George, a manure agent, lived in the house on the right adjacent to the road junction. By 1914 Alfred Longbottom was the proprietor of 'James Mitchell'. In 1922 the manure agent had departed and a furniture dealer occupied the premises. By 1935 it was the Omega Café. An advert dated 1914 for James Mitchell, civil and military tailors, announced that they were agents for Burberry garments and supplied liveries, costumes, breeches, hats and chauffeurs' uniforms. The house has ornate stonework with turned pillars and is of a mid-Victorian design.

In 1969 when Edgar Street was widened to make way for the trunk road many buildings were demolished, among them Clarence House which was perhaps one of the finest. The area is now part of the road and in 1991 it was widened to four lanes to improve traffic flow.

This print taken from a broken glass negative is of Eign Street about 1910. The painted sign of Pilleys Cafe where J. Dorey was proprietor is visible on the wall above the entrance. Next door the sign above Turners shop reads 'Boots for Farm, Field, Town & Country & Kyrle Boots'. The Three Crowns Inn owned by the Hereford and Tredegar Brewery Ltd with its curved dormer windows is visible. To the right of the picture is Eign Street Post Office run by Wilson and Phillips who published postcards of Hereford.

This was one of the city's first streets to be closed to traffic in 1969 when it was paved and trees planted. The painted signs on the walls have gone. It is worth noticing the increased twist on the All Saints church spire.

At the turn of the century Hereford had over 30 butchers shops. Most would have had two or more workers so the trade was a fairly substantial employer. The old Butter Market had ten butchers. Without refrigeration one wonders how long the meat could be stored. This photograph is of Nelsons shop about 1912. Mr Nelson is just visible inside and his sons outside. The whole display is labelled 'Prime New Season's Lamb' and 'fresh supplies daily'. Note the son with the long bladed knife and also the gas lamp with its on and off pull strings. The shop was in Eign Street.

The building survives today as a café, and during the summer months tables and chairs are put out on the pedestrian street giving a continental look to the area.

Opposite: The Victoria Eye and Ear Hospital was established under the name Herefordshire and South Wales Eye and Ear Institution in July 1882. This building in Eign Street was opened on 29th August 1889. This photograph was taken about 1910, when the Hospital had beds for 20 patients and 2,000 outpatients were seen each year.

The building has now been cleaned and is free of the extensive growth of ivy which no doubt reduced the light inside. The old entrance and porch has been very well disguised by inserting a window frame and old bricks up to sill level. Out of view to the right of the photograph, a modern operating theatre extension has been added.

Here is a photograph taken by Jean O'Donell just prior to the building of the inner relief road in 1967. The building on the left is part of Edwards, hairdressers. The more distant light coloured building was originally the Eign Gate Inn, later renamed the Maidenhead Inn. At the time of this picture it was Charles Parry's butchers shop. Next door can be seen Kings radio and cycle shop. The 'mock' timber framed building, built early this century is the Red Lion Hotel, while to the right with a curved front is Gardiner's confectionery shop. Behind was Deans grocery stores. The wall to the right belonged to Bewell House, the Hereford, Tredegar and Cheltenham Brewery offices. Just round the corner near the mini van, was Horace Webb a gunsmith. Note the policeman on point duty near the Red Lion.

The loss of all buildings except 'Sylvia Stylists' has changed the perspective. The Red Lion flats are on the left and Steels on the right, both of which are now city landmarks. The view along Eign Street is clearly seen.

This is the Old Plough Inn on the corner of Whitecross Road and Plough Lane. Its coach house is seen along Plough Lane which leads to Canon Moor Farm and the Midland Railway Inn. In 1934 it was listed as Ye Old Plough Inn run by Mrs Rosa Bailey. By 1955 Mr Woodward was the new landlord and along the lane near Canon Moor Farm, Sweetman & Son hauliers, Hereford Petroleum Co. and Asphalt Public Works were operating. Until the last war Whitecross Street ran from Eign Street to Prices Almshouses and from Whitehorse Street onwards was Whitecross Road.

This is an excellent example of how a replacement building has enhanced an area. The new building is of a mock half timbered and brick construction. The satellite dish represents the latest TV technology.

The Whitecross was originally built by Bishop Charlton (1361–70) and restored in 1864. William Collins, in his *Historical Landmarks of Hereford 1915* suggests that the cross was built when the Black Death swept the county and carried away half the population. Today however, all stories associated with the erection of the cross are dismissed as myths but it is known that during the plague citizens deposited their money in basins filled with vinegar then retreated, while the country folk advanced, took the money and left its value in eggs, butter, poultry and vegetables. The original monument was a six-sided pedestal with panels on eight steps with a cross. In 1864, it was restored by the Rt Hon and Ven Lord Saye and Seale, one of the canons of the cathedral. This photograph, taken by Walter Pritchard in 1904, is of a 1903 Minerva motorcycle with its owner Mr C. S. Chubb. This is one of the oldest photographs of a motorcycle in Hereford.

This fairly recent photograph of the late Mr A. H. Foxton with the same motorcycle re-enacts the original picture. He bought and restored the old motorcycle which is now as good as new.

This is a picture postcard which was posted in 1943 during the last war. It shows a part of the RAF camp at Credenhill adjacent to the main road. This photograph must have been passed by the censors since military pictures were never used in such a way during wartime. The camp was built in 1940 in under six months. The huts in the photograph were used as the medical centre. Just visible is a water tower above the roof line. The RAF camp which opened in 1940 was occupied by three technical training schools. The late A. H. Foxton, who was one of the very first instructors, remembered that the water supply was very polluted when first used and caused widespread illness in the camp. Note the profusion of telephone and electricity posts.

It is now well over 50 years since the military 'temporary' wooden huts were built for the last war. They have survived in good condition. However this view is not quite the same since married quarters now occupy the original site slightly to the left.

In the middle Victorian period Hereford had three Railway Stations — Moorfields for trains to Hay on Wye, Barton for Newport and Abergavenny, and Barrs Court for Shrewsbury and Worcester. In the early days the different railway companies were deadly rivals but eventually, mainly for financial reasons, they amalgamated or reached agreement on running over another company's rails so that there was no need for three stations in the city. The Barton Station seen in this picture was closed to passenger traffic in 1893 following an agreement for the Midland Railway to use Barrs Court. Barton survived for freight use until 1979.

Little now remains of the original view except the distant house. The car park is on the old station site, and even the old Whitecross Street railway bridge was recently removed and a pedestrian tunnel inserted. This was done prior to the opening of the nearby Sainsbury's supermarket.

Henry Percival Bulmer, born on 28th February 1867, was the son of a parson. In 1887 aged 20 he started to make perry and cider from the Credenhill Glebe Orchard using a stone mill on a neighbours farm. At the end of the year he moved to a warehouse in Maylord Street next to the old *Hereford Times* building and that autumn produced 4,000 gallons. In August 1888 the family purchased an acre of land in Ryeland Street for £350. This photograph taken in 1934 shows part of a large consignment of pomagne heading for the USA at the railway sidings behind the Ryelands Street factory.

In recent years rail freight has declined, and many goods yards have been developed for housing and industry. Here the Barton railway yard has been made into a business estate which includes a British Telecom exchange, Sainsbury's supermarket, the City Council depot, a social club, and some housing. The picture was taken from a high level with the roof of the Council depot and archaeology unit in the foreground.

Hereford has been a centre for transport since possibly Roman times. There was a ford below the Bishops Palace which was a meeting place for several roads. Horses had been the main source of motive power until the arrival of steam and petrol, and this new power has given us speed and freedom. Here we see the Midland Red staff at their garage in 1929 with three new buses. The Birmingham and Midland Omnibus Company had their garage in Friar Street next to Watkins Bros. who were millers. The buses were made by Tilling Stevens and are TS3 models with a Birmingham registration number plate.

Hereford was one of the last towns in the West Midlands to have a 'hopper' bus service. This photograph was taken at the Friar Street garage in August 1991 with two hopper vehicles, and an older bus in the centre. In the picture from the left are Sean Pratt, Arthur Jones, Les Spencer and Brian Stevens, the garage fitter.

In 1904 the motor car was considered to be smelly, noisy, expensive and unreliable. The Automobile Club (now RAC) promoted a national six day motoring endurance trial in Hereford to show the public that this was not so and arranged for the entrants to travel two laps of a 50 mile course each day for six days to make a total distance of 600 miles. The route was changed each day. Seen on the photograph taken near the Imperial Flour Mills, Friar Street, is car No. 17 a 7hp Alldays which had a total of eight non-stop runs out of 12. Just visible is car No. 25 described in the programme as a new type Oldsmobile. Hereford was chosen as a centre for this car trial because it had its own automobile club which could provide organisers and the routes could include such hills as Dinmore and Fromes Hill. This was the first large trial for the small motor car in the country and it received national publicity. The overall winner was a 6hp Siddeley which ran non-stop — a considerable achievement when roads were often rough, muddy and littered with many horse shoe nails. Note the high roof line of the flour mills and chimney.

The old building which was in front of the flour mills, a part of the Drill Hall, has been replaced by the Hereford Military Club. Note the loss of the chimney and cottages in the distance. The car park remains — nearly 90 years on.

Over the years a few Hereford residents have taken their own photographs of events etc. in the city, usually with simple cameras. These photographs taken by the late Mr G. Lewin of Bridge Street, show the Barton Tavern in St Nicholas Street at different states of demoliton during 1968. The viewpoints are mostly from the Barton Road near St Nicholas Church. Nearby stood the old city gate called Friars Gate. The old road sign reads City Centre to the left and Ross, Abergavenny to the right.

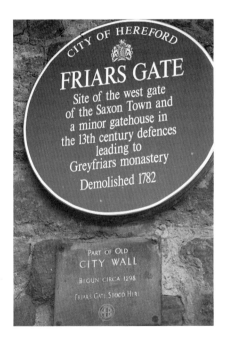

Today, after only 21 years the view is almost unrecognisable. First the new Wye bridge and approach road were built and a year ago the new block of retirement flats 'Deans Court' was finished. This is considered by some to be poor development on a very sensitive and historical site.

This is the Residence Hotel photographed from King Street about 1955. The Aubrey Street junction is in front of the Heinz advertisement. To the left is Thomas Perry's motor accessories shop where he also sold BP petrol. The pumps are visible in the middle of his front window. The storage tanks were probably in the cellar, and one does wonder just what the fire risk was. A large coach house stands behind the Heinz and Cadburys signs and an ancient timber frame building is also visible. The main frontage for the Residence Hotel is in Broad Street. The tall buildings in the background are part of the library, museum and art gallery. The wall advertising was changed regularly by the Hereford and Monmouth Advertising Company who were at 20 Commercial Road.

The jumble of outbuildings has gone and the replacement building 'Thorpe House' has a corner frontage from Aubrey Street to Broad Street.

Herefordshire General Hospital. Hawkins Ward.

Until the 18th Century the sick and poor in Hereford were mainly helped by monks and a few doctors. In the mid-18th Century some individuals funded the foundation of our General Hospital when none existed in Wales. The founder of the Hereford General Infirmary was the Rev Thomas Talbot of Ullingswick. He contributed a substantial £500 towards this in 1775. In November the Earl of Oxford donated a site on the river bank for the infirmary and a temporary building was opened in 1776 which was used for 7½ years. Among the original subscribers was Mrs Joan Hawkins who paid £200. This postcard view of the Hawkins Ward dates from about 1920. Note the grand piano.

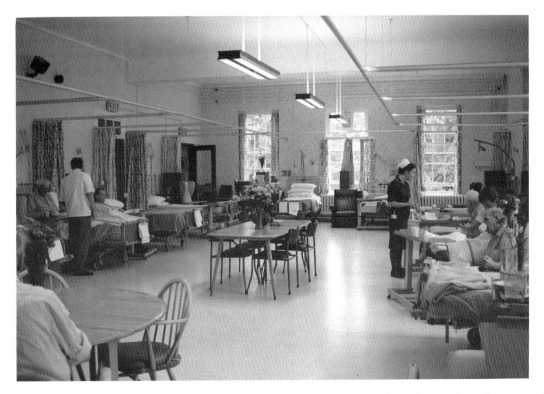

This photograph clearly shows how a ward in a general hospital has changed. Patients can be screened with curtains for privacy, each bed is fully adjustable, the smooth floor surface easily cleaned and radio and power points are next to each bed. The windows give a pleasant view over the River Wye and King George playing fields. There are proposals to build a new hospital at Burghill which should open in about eight years.

Opposite: Newspapers, cards, toys etc. can be seen on this 1915 postcard of Mills shop in Bridge Street. The following newspaper headlines are clear enough to read. *Daily Chronicle* — Paris threatened with famine and darkness. *Daily Mail* — Astonishing development of naval crisis. *Daily Mirror* — King Edward attends races at Biarritz. The *Daily News* announced — Co-operative housing: Interesting scheme for Hereford, while the *Daily Express* — Cabinet and Navy 'fiddled' while presumably Rome burns. Mrs Mills is on the right with her assistant. Note the large exterior gas lamp. The shop to the right, on the corner of Bridge Street and St Nicholas Street, was occupied in 1915 by Walter Williams, a pharmaceutical chemist, but by 1935 had changed hands to Lewis-Smith, chemist. The second photograph is of Mr George Lewin's shop about 1958. The *Daily Mail* and *Express* both have posterboards outside. It is interesting to see his shop front looks much older than that of Mr Mills.

The 'shop' remains but now it is a part of a solicitors business. Today solicitors expand into new pastures and here they sell property which was not possible only a few years ago.

The River Wye, which has many rapids and shallow areas, was not used extensively for transport of goods but during high water river barges were used to carry freight up and down stream from the city. In Hereford, the river has been used for pleasure for very many years by small boats. In the 1880's a small steam powered boat was used regularly. This photograph, though faded and not sharp, is however a superb rare glimpse of a small sailing boat taken near Jordans Boat Yard about 1880. The boat man dressed in his waistcoat and boater is using a long pole to push the boat out into the river. Note the two small boys on board.

When Jordans Boat Yard was demolished to make way for the new bridge, Hereford lost its only boat hire business. Last year Frank Barton brought a River Rhine barge, 125 feet long, up the Wye and also started a summer pleasure boat service from the bank adjacent to the old boat yard. In the photograph is Madeline James who has the only Department of Transport Class 5 boat licence for taking pleasure boats on the River Wye. The river banks for half a mile on either side of the Wye Bridge have common mooring rights.

This photograph of Cross Street to the right, and Belmont Road was taken by a member of the Quinsey family. It shows a tranquil scene, and several timber framed cottages. In 1915 the shop on the corner was recorded as being 11 Belmont Road owned by Charles Quinsey, a fish and fruit dealer. The shop in the background was owned by Charles Brown a baker and grocer. In 1935 the bakery was occupied by Harold Craddock and Henry J. Quinsey was in the corner shop.

The whole block that occupied the area between Belmont Road, Ross Road and Cross Street was demolished to make way for a road junction with the new bridge approach. The roundabout is unable to cope with the traffic at peak hours leading to long delays.

The old buildings were demolished before 1895 as the ordnance survey map for that year shows no record of them. The modern version of Drybridge House retains its original fascia.

Opposite top: Hereford had several turnpikes but all were removed in 1870 when they were abolished. This postcard picture would therefore be dated before 1869. The turnpike would collect the toll which went towards the upkeep of that particular section of highway. The photograph was taken on a quiet day, since no vehicles are visible and the toll keeper has time to talk to the pedestrians. His chickens run on the road searching for food. Note how the gas lamp is positioned so that it illuminates the area and ensures that people cannot pass without payment at night. The large house in the background is the old Drybridge House while the house on the left is the tollkeepers cottage.

Opposite bottom: There are some occupied parts of Hereford which have a long history of flooding. This postcard view is of St Martins Street taken from the junction with Ross Road and Belmont Road. Here is an AA patrol man wearing his long motorcycle boots and a police constable looking past the photographer. In the distance a Wye Valley Motors bus returns to its garage just round the corner. The building to the right is the Crown Inn where Frank Waters was landlord. In the cottage on the left, No. 37, was George Jones. At the far end of the terrace was the Shell Mex & BP depot. Note the large overhead gas lamp. Compare this picture with the old St Martins Turnpike picture above it. The cottages behind the turnpike appear on both photographs and identify the location.

After exceptional heavy rain or snow in the Welsh mountains the River Wye will flood low lying land. After a winter of heavy snow this photograph shows the result on the Belmont Road outside Pool Farm. The car, possibly a Standard, later would have had an expensive visit to the garage to return it to good working order. Pool Farm was described by William Collins in his book *Historical Landmarks of Hereford 1915*, as having a porch, and dates from the early 17th century. Though the marks of age are only too visible, enough remains to show its Stuart dignity and beauty. The proportions are good and the design simple and effective. In the photograph next to the farm two new shops are seen and on the extreme right is Causeway Farm.

The spectacular deep floods of old have not been seen for many years, the recent ones being relatively minor. Note the loss of Causeway Farm.

Here is a postcard view taken on Belmont Road of the Causeway Farm during floods in 1912. The old donkey which is pulling the cart with two elderly ladies, seems undisturbed by the water. The floods have brought out many local residents to watch the vehicles on their way into Hereford. Causeway Farm was described in Collins' *Historical Landmarks of Hereford* as 'of the Tudor period, slightly modernised with some of its ancient beauty still left'. The farmer in 1905 was Thomas Watkins. The timber framed cottage in the background is Pool Farm.

Recent floods have been fairly shallow in this area. The only old building left is Pool Farm. The 'new' buildings incorporate shops with living accommodation over, and a disused garage which, with its associated land, extends almost to the river bank. We await proposals for its future use.

The old Ship Inn photograph was taken in the early 1930's with the 'regulars', none of whom can be identified. The present landlord Jim Winters kindly loaned this photograph.

The Ship Inn was rebuilt about 1938 to a classical public house design with mock half timber, and leaded glass windows.

Old photographs taken inside pubs are very rare. This picture remained unidentified for a long time until it was recognised as being inside the Ship Inn, Ross Road. The small sailing boat seen in the leaded window was the clue. This is a Geoffrey Hammonds photograph and was taken in 1948. It is a glimpse of the 'working man' in the public bar relaxing with the inevitable pint of beer. Note that most men had a 'flat' hat. The only person who can be identified is Bill Gretton who has his back to the fireplace.

The Saturday lunch time regulars seen here are 'Cess' Knight, Sylvia Causer, Ernie Causer, Martin Mellish and Sigmund Müller. Note that caps and ties are absent, and the fireplace has been carefully boxed in and central heating installed.

At the turn of the century the residential areas of Hereford extended almost to Lower Bullingham. The building to the left is the church attached to St Elizabeth's School. The school was established by the Sisters of Charity who moved to Rotherwas House in 1861 and into Morelands, Bullingham a year later, when a girls' orphanage was started. By 1870 boys were recorded as being in residence. In 1867 a departing local farmer gave the Sisters his empty house and it was re-named St Elizabeth's School. A large wing was built in 1875 and converted into a mixed school. The chapel was also built in 1875 and a church in 1906. At the outbreak of the Second World War the Sisters and pupils were evacuated to Croft Castle.

In June 1950 the school buildings with three acres were sold for £2,000 to the Polish Catholic Church represented by four Clerks in Holy Orders. The building adjacent to the church is a residential home for Polish refugees. Today the road is very busy, being a main road to the Rotherwas Industrial Estate. The proposed by-pass will help considerably, if built.

Dinedor Tea Gardens were at the top of Dinedor hill a mile outside the city boundary. On Sundays during good weather many city inhabitants would walk up to the top of the hill for the view and no doubt a cup of tea. Here we see numerous visitors and girls with tea trays. The owner in 1905 was Frank Harrison of Dinedor Camp. A short while later it was run by Mr Holmes who leased the building from the County Council. His family ran it for some 50 years.

Today the cottage has been extended and is now used by the County Council Youth services. Hereford resident Mrs Doris Jenkins who is now over 80, recalled that during the last war workers from the surrounding fields below arrived at the tea rooms for cigarettes and mineral waters. However the tea gardens were closed in 1960 because of lack of council funds to modernise the kitchens to comply with hygiene regulations. Now the gardens are all lawn, and outside toilet blocks have been built for the campers which include school groups and scouts.

List of Places and Events